EMMANUEL JOSEPH

The Architect of Abundance, Building Empires That Outlast Generations

Copyright © 2025 by Emmanuel Joseph

All rights reserved. No part of this publication may be reproduced, stored or transmitted in any form or by any means, electronic, mechanical, photocopying, recording, scanning, or otherwise without written permission from the publisher. It is illegal to copy this book, post it to a website, or distribute it by any other means without permission.

First edition

This book was professionally typeset on Reedsy.
Find out more at reedsy.com

Contents

1	Chapter 1: Introduction: The Vision of Legacy	1
2	Chapter 2: Foundations of Wealth: The First Bricks	3
3	Chapter 3: Embracing Innovation: The Path Forward	5
4	Chapter 4: Strategic Growth: Expanding Horizons	7
5	Chapter 5: People Power: Building a Cohesive Team	9
6	Chapter 6: Sustainable Practices: The Long-Term View	11
7	Chapter 7: Ethical Leadership: Guiding with Integrity	13
8	Chapter 8: Diversification: Spreading the Roots	15
9	Chapter 9: Technological Mastery: Leveraging Advancements	17
10	Chapter 10: Resilience: Thriving in Adversity	19
11	Chapter 11: Nurturing Relationships: The Core of Networking	21
12	Chapter 12: Legacy Planning: Preparing the Next Generation	23
13	Chapter 13: Community Engagement: Creating Social Impact	25
14	Chapter 14: Financial Acumen: Mastering Money Management	27
15	Chapter 15: Visionary Thinking: Anticipating the Future	29
16	Chapter 16: Cultural Influence: Shaping the Zeitgeist	31
17	Chapter 17: Conclusion: The Eternal Blueprint	33

1

Chapter 1: Introduction: The Vision of Legacy

In the serene twilight of his life, Nathaniel knew that the legacy he left behind would be his true testament. His empire, built on the bedrock of passion, innovation, and unyielding determination, stood tall against the horizon, a testament to what visionary thinking could accomplish. To Nathaniel, wealth was never about the accumulation of riches; it was about creating a foundation that would outlast his mortal existence. As he gazed upon the skyline, each tower, each structure, represented a fragment of his journey—a journey fueled by a desire to create abundance not just for himself, but for generations to come.

The vision of legacy is not born overnight. It is a seed planted in the fertile soil of dreams, watered by the sweat of hard work, and nurtured by the relentless pursuit of excellence. The architect of abundance sees beyond the immediate gains and focuses on the impact of their endeavors on future generations. This book delves into the principles and practices that form the blueprint for building an enduring empire. From the initial spark of an idea to the intricacies of strategic growth, we will explore the journey of turning dreams into reality.

One of the fundamental pillars of building an empire is the recognition of one's purpose. Purpose gives direction, fuels passion, and provides the strength to persevere through challenges. It is the beacon that guides the architect through the stormy seas of uncertainty, steering the ship towards the shores of success. In this chapter, we will uncover the elements that shape a compelling vision and the importance of aligning one's goals with their core values. A well-defined purpose is the cornerstone upon which empires are built, and it serves as a constant reminder of why the journey began in the first place.

Moreover, the vision of legacy encompasses not just financial prosperity, but also the cultivation of values, principles, and a sense of responsibility towards the community. The architect of abundance understands that true wealth lies in the impact one has on the world around them. By fostering a culture of integrity, innovation, and inclusivity, they lay the groundwork for a thriving and sustainable empire. As we embark on this exploration, we will draw insights from history, modern-day success stories, and timeless wisdom to illustrate how visionary leaders have crafted their legacies.

2

Chapter 2: Foundations of Wealth: The First Bricks

The journey to building an enduring empire begins with laying the right foundations. The initial steps taken in the early stages of business can significantly impact long-term success. The architect of abundance understands that patience, diligence, and a keen eye for detail are essential in this phase. The cornerstone of a prosperous empire is a solid business model, one that is not only financially viable but also aligned with the founder's vision and values.

In this chapter, we explore the importance of thorough market research and the identification of opportunities that align with the founder's strengths and passions. By understanding the market landscape, the architect can make informed decisions that minimize risks and maximize potential returns. Additionally, the significance of building a strong brand identity from the outset cannot be overstated. A compelling brand story resonates with customers, creating a loyal following that will support the business through its growth phases.

Financial prudence is another critical aspect of laying the foundations of wealth. Effective budgeting, prudent investment, and maintaining a healthy cash flow are essential to ensure the business remains resilient during turbulent times. The architect of abundance understands that financial discipline in the early stages sets the stage for sustainable growth and long-term success. In this chapter, we delve into the strategies for managing finances effectively and the importance of seeking expert advice when necessary.

Moreover, the foundation of wealth is not just about financial capital but also about human capital. Building a team of talented, motivated, and aligned individuals is crucial for the success of any enterprise. The architect of abundance prioritizes creating a positive work culture that fosters innovation, collaboration, and personal growth. We will explore the principles of effective team-building and the role of leadership in nurturing a thriving organizational culture.

3

Chapter 3: Embracing Innovation: The Path Forward

Innovation is the lifeblood of any enduring empire. The architect of abundance recognizes that staying ahead of the curve requires a constant pursuit of new ideas, technologies, and methodologies. In a rapidly changing world, the ability to adapt and innovate is what sets successful enterprises apart from those that falter. This chapter delves into the mindset and strategies necessary for fostering a culture of innovation within an organization.

Embracing innovation begins with a willingness to challenge the status quo and explore uncharted territories. The architect of abundance encourages a mindset of curiosity and open-mindedness, where team members feel empowered to experiment, take risks, and learn from failures. By creating an environment that celebrates creativity and values diverse perspectives, the organization becomes a breeding ground for groundbreaking ideas.

One of the key components of innovation is the strategic integration of technology. In this chapter, we explore how emerging technologies can be leveraged to streamline operations, enhance customer experiences, and create new revenue streams. The architect of abundance stays informed about technological advancements and is proactive in adopting tools and systems that drive efficiency and competitiveness. We will examine case studies of organizations that have successfully harnessed technology to revolutionize their industries.

Additionally, innovation extends beyond products and services to encompass business processes, organizational structures, and market strategies. The architect of abundance continuously seeks ways to optimize and improve every aspect of the business. By fostering a culture of continuous improvement and staying attuned to industry trends, the organization remains agile and responsive to changing market dynamics.

4

Chapter 4: Strategic Growth: Expanding Horizons

Growth is an essential aspect of building an empire, but not all growth is created equal. The architect of abundance understands that strategic growth, driven by well-informed decisions and deliberate actions, is the key to long-term success. In this chapter, we delve into the principles of strategic growth and the steps necessary to expand horizons while maintaining stability.

The foundation of strategic growth lies in a clear and well-defined growth strategy. The architect of abundance sets specific, measurable, achievable, relevant, and time-bound (SMART) goals that align with the organization's vision and values. These goals serve as a roadmap, guiding the organization through its expansion journey. In this chapter, we explore the process of setting SMART goals and the importance of regularly reviewing and adjusting them as needed.

One of the critical aspects of strategic growth is market expansion. The architect of abundance identifies new markets and customer segments that align with the organization's strengths and capabilities. This involves conducting thorough market research, understanding customer needs, and tailoring products and services to meet those needs. We will examine case studies of successful market expansion strategies and the lessons learned from both triumphs and challenges.

Moreover, strategic growth involves scaling operations in a way that maintains quality and efficiency. The architect of abundance invests in infrastructure, technology, and talent to support the organization's growth trajectory. This chapter delves into the strategies for managing operational scalability, including optimizing supply chains, enhancing production capabilities, and maintaining customer satisfaction during periods of rapid growth.

5

Chapter 5: People Power: Building a Cohesive Team

At the heart of every successful empire lies a team of dedicated and talented individuals. The architect of abundance understands that a cohesive team, united by a common vision and shared values, is essential for achieving greatness. This chapter explores the principles of effective team-building and the role of leadership in creating a thriving organizational culture.

Building a cohesive team begins with hiring individuals who not only possess the necessary skills and expertise but also align with the organization's core values and vision. The architect of abundance prioritizes cultural fit and fosters an environment where team members feel valued, respected, and empowered to contribute their best. In this chapter, we delve into the strategies for attracting and retaining top talent, as well as the importance of diversity and inclusion in driving innovation and creativity.

Effective communication is the glue that binds a team together. The architect of abundance fosters open and transparent communication channels, ensuring that team members feel heard and understood. By promoting a culture of collaboration and feedback, the organization can harness the collective wisdom and creativity of its people. We will explore the principles of effective communication and the tools and techniques that facilitate seamless collaboration within a team.

Moreover, leadership plays a crucial role in building and sustaining a cohesive team. The architect of abundance leads by example, demonstrating integrity, empathy, and resilience. They inspire and motivate their team, providing guidance and support while empowering individuals to take ownership of their roles. This chapter delves into the qualities of effective leadership and the importance of continuous learning and development for both leaders and team members.

6

Chapter 6: Sustainable Practices: The Long-Term View

Sustainability is a key consideration for any empire that aims to endure through generations. The architect of abundance recognizes the importance of adopting sustainable practices that benefit not only the business but also the environment and society as a whole. This chapter explores the principles of sustainability and the steps necessary to build a business that thrives in harmony with its surroundings.

Sustainable practices begin with a commitment to responsible resource management. The architect of abundance implements strategies to minimize waste, conserve energy, and reduce the organization's carbon footprint. By adopting eco-friendly practices and investing in renewable energy sources, the organization can contribute to environmental preservation while also reaping financial benefits in the long run. In this chapter, we examine case studies of organizations that have successfully integrated sustainability into their operations and the positive impact it has had on their bottom line.

Moreover, sustainability extends to the social dimension, encompassing fair labor practices, community engagement, and ethical sourcing. The architect of abundance prioritizes the well-being of employees, suppliers, and local communities, ensuring that their business practices promote social equity and economic development. We will explore the principles of corporate social responsibility and the importance of creating shared value for all stakeholders.

Sustainable practices also involve a long-term perspective on business growth and development. The architect of abundance understands that short-term gains should not come at the expense of long-term stability. By adopting a holistic approach to decision-making and considering the broader impact of their actions, the organization can build a resilient and sustainable empire. This chapter delves into the strategies for balancing short-term and long-term goals and the importance of continuous innovation and improvement.

7

Chapter 7: Ethical Leadership: Guiding with Integrity

Ethical leadership is the cornerstone of an enduring empire. The architect of abundance leads with integrity, setting the tone for the entire organization and fostering a culture of trust and accountability. This chapter explores the principles of ethical leadership and the importance of guiding an organization with a strong moral compass.

Ethical leadership begins with a commitment to honesty, transparency, and fairness. The architect of abundance upholds high ethical standards and ensures that these values are embedded in every aspect of the business. By demonstrating ethical behavior and holding themselves and others accountable, leaders can build a culture of trust and respect. In this chapter, we delve into the qualities of ethical leadership and the role of ethical decision-making in building a sustainable and successful empire.

Moreover, ethical leadership involves a commitment to social and environmental responsibility. The architect of abundance recognizes that businesses have a responsibility to contribute positively to society and the planet. By adopting ethical business practices and prioritizing sustainability, leaders can create a positive impact that extends beyond the organization. We will explore the principles of corporate ethics and the importance of aligning business practices with broader social and environmental goals.

Ethical leadership also requires a focus on the well-being and development of employees. The architect of abundance prioritizes the growth and development of their team, providing opportunities for learning, advancement, and personal fulfillment. By fostering a supportive and inclusive work environment, leaders can inspire and motivate their team to achieve their best. This chapter delves into the strategies for creating a culture of ethical leadership and the importance of continuous improvement and self-reflection.

8

Chapter 8: Diversification: Spreading the Roots

Diversification is a crucial strategy for building a resilient and enduring empire. The architect of abundance understands the importance of spreading risk and exploring new opportunities to ensure long-term stability and growth. This chapter explores the principles of diversification and the steps necessary to expand an organization's horizons.

Diversification begins with a thorough understanding of the organization's strengths and capabilities. The architect of abundance identifies areas where the organization can leverage its existing expertise to enter new markets or develop new products and services. By diversifying their offerings, the organization can reduce its reliance on a single revenue stream and increase its resilience to market fluctuations. In this chapter, we examine case studies of successful diversification strategies and the lessons learned from both successes and challenges.

Moreover, diversification involves exploring new markets and customer segments. The architect of abundance conducts thorough market research to identify opportunities that align with the organization's vision and values. By understanding customer needs and tailoring offerings to meet those needs, the organization can tap into new sources of growth. We will explore the principles of market diversification and the strategies for entering new markets successfully.

Diversification also extends to investments and financial management. The architect of abundance adopts a diversified investment portfolio, balancing risk and return to ensure long-term financial stability. By investing in a mix of assets, the organization can mitigate the impact of market volatility and achieve sustainable growth. This chapter delves into the principles of investment diversification and the importance of prudent financial management.

9

Chapter 9: Technological Mastery: Leveraging Advancements

In an era defined by rapid technological advancements, the architect of abundance understands the importance of staying at the forefront of innovation. Leveraging technology can significantly enhance operational efficiency, customer experience, and overall competitiveness. This chapter explores the principles of technological mastery and the steps necessary to harness the power of technology for long-term success.

Technological mastery begins with a commitment to continuous learning and adaptation. The architect of abundance stays informed about emerging technologies and trends, ensuring that the organization is well-positioned to capitalize on new opportunities. By fostering a culture of innovation and encouraging team members to embrace new tools and systems, the organization can remain agile and responsive to change. In this chapter, we delve into the strategies for staying ahead of the technological curve and the importance of investing in research and development.

Moreover, technological mastery involves integrating technology seamlessly into every aspect of the business. From automating routine tasks to enhancing customer interactions through artificial intelligence, the architect of abundance leverages technology to create value and drive growth. We will explore case studies of organizations that have successfully integrated technology into their operations and the positive impact it has had on their bottom line.

Furthermore, technological mastery extends to data-driven decision-making. The architect of abundance understands the importance of harnessing data to gain insights, identify trends, and make informed decisions. By implementing robust data analytics systems and fostering a data-driven culture, the organization can optimize performance and drive innovation. This chapter delves into the principles of data-driven decision-making and the tools and techniques that facilitate effective data analysis.

10

Chapter 10: Resilience: Thriving in Adversity

Resilience is a critical quality for any empire that aims to endure through generations. The architect of abundance recognizes that challenges and setbacks are inevitable, and the ability to adapt and thrive in the face of adversity is what sets successful enterprises apart. This chapter explores the principles of resilience and the steps necessary to build a business that can weather storms and emerge stronger.

Resilience begins with a mindset of adaptability and flexibility. The architect of abundance embraces change and views challenges as opportunities for growth and learning. By fostering a culture of resilience and encouraging team members to develop a growth mindset, the organization can navigate uncertainty with confidence. In this chapter, we delve into the strategies for cultivating resilience within an organization and the importance of maintaining a positive and proactive attitude.

Moreover, resilience involves building a robust and agile infrastructure. The architect of abundance invests in systems and processes that enhance the organization's ability to respond to changes in the market, supply chain disruptions, and other unforeseen events. By prioritizing operational efficiency and maintaining a diversified portfolio, the organization can mitigate risks and ensure long-term stability. We will examine case studies of organizations that have demonstrated resilience in the face of adversity and the lessons learned from their experiences.

Furthermore, resilience extends to financial management and contingency planning. The architect of abundance adopts prudent financial practices, including maintaining healthy cash reserves and diversifying revenue streams, to ensure the organization remains resilient during economic downturns. This chapter delves into the principles of financial resilience and the importance of proactive risk management.

11

Chapter 11: Nurturing Relationships: The Core of Networking

Strong relationships and a robust network are vital components of an enduring empire. The architect of abundance understands that success is not achieved in isolation but through collaboration and mutual support. This chapter explores the principles of nurturing relationships and the importance of building a strong network.

Nurturing relationships begins with a genuine commitment to building trust and rapport. The architect of abundance prioritizes authentic connections and invests time and effort in understanding the needs and aspirations of others. By demonstrating empathy, respect, and integrity, they foster relationships that are built on a foundation of mutual trust and respect. In this chapter, we delve into the strategies for building and maintaining strong relationships and the importance of effective communication and active listening.

Moreover, networking extends beyond personal relationships to encompass strategic partnerships and alliances. The architect of abundance identifies opportunities for collaboration and seeks out partners who share their vision and values. By leveraging the strengths and resources of strategic partners, the organization can achieve greater success and create shared value. We will explore case studies of successful partnerships and the lessons learned from both triumphs and challenges.

Furthermore, nurturing relationships involves a commitment to giving back and creating value for others. The architect of abundance recognizes that a strong network is built on reciprocity and mutual support. By contributing to the success and well-being of others, they create a positive and supportive community that fosters growth and innovation. This chapter delves into the principles of giving back and the importance of creating a culture of generosity and support.

12

Chapter 12: Legacy Planning: Preparing the Next Generation

An enduring empire is built with the future in mind. The architect of abundance understands the importance of preparing the next generation to carry forward the vision and values of the organization. This chapter explores the principles of legacy planning and the steps necessary to ensure a seamless transition of leadership and responsibility.

Legacy planning begins with a clear and well-defined succession plan. The architect of abundance identifies potential leaders within the organization and invests in their development and growth. By providing opportunities for learning, mentorship, and leadership development, they ensure that the next generation is well-equipped to take on future challenges and responsibilities. In this chapter, we delve into the strategies for effective succession planning and the importance of nurturing leadership talent.

Moreover, legacy planning involves instilling the organization's vision and values in the next generation. The architect of abundance prioritizes creating a strong organizational culture that reflects the core principles and aspirations of the founder. By fostering a sense of purpose and commitment among future leaders, they ensure that the organization's legacy is preserved and carried forward. We will explore the principles of value-based leadership and the importance of creating a culture of continuity and stability.

Furthermore, legacy planning extends to financial and estate planning. The architect of abundance adopts prudent financial practices and ensures that the organization's assets and resources are managed and preserved for future generations. This chapter delves into the principles of financial legacy planning and the importance of proactive estate management.

13

Chapter 13: Community Engagement: Creating Social Impact

Community engagement is a key aspect of building an enduring empire. The architect of abundance recognizes the importance of giving back to the community and creating a positive social impact. This chapter explores the principles of community engagement and the steps necessary to build meaningful connections with the community.

Community engagement begins with a commitment to understanding the needs and aspirations of the community. The architect of abundance invests time and effort in building relationships with community members and stakeholders, listening to their concerns and identifying opportunities for collaboration. By demonstrating empathy and a genuine commitment to creating value, the organization can build trust and support within the community. In this chapter, we delve into the strategies for effective community engagement and the importance of active listening and collaboration.

Moreover, community engagement involves contributing to the social and economic well-being of the community. The architect of abundance prioritizes initiatives that create positive social impact, such as supporting local education, healthcare, and economic development. By investing in initiatives that align with the organization's vision and values, the organization can create shared value and contribute to the long-term prosperity of the community. We will explore case studies of successful community engagement initiatives and the lessons learned from both triumphs and challenges.

Furthermore, community engagement extends to corporate social responsibility (CSR) and sustainability initiatives. The architect of abundance adopts ethical business practices and prioritizes sustainability, ensuring that their operations contribute positively to the environment and society. This chapter delves into the principles of CSR and sustainability and the importance of aligning business practices with broader social and environmental goals.

14

Chapter 14: Financial Acumen: Mastering Money Management

Financial acumen is a critical skill for building an enduring empire. The architect of abundance understands the importance of mastering money management and making informed financial decisions. This chapter explores the principles of financial acumen and the steps necessary to build a financially stable and prosperous organization.

Financial acumen begins with a thorough understanding of the organization's financial health. The architect of abundance prioritizes accurate financial reporting and analysis, ensuring that they have a clear and comprehensive view of the organization's financial position. By regularly reviewing financial statements and key performance indicators, the organization can identify opportunities for improvement and make informed decisions. In this chapter, we delve into the strategies for effective financial analysis and the importance of maintaining accurate financial records.

Moreover, financial acumen involves prudent budgeting and resource allocation. The architect of abundance adopts a disciplined approach to budgeting, ensuring that resources are allocated efficiently and effectively to support the organization's goals. By prioritizing investments that generate long-term value and avoiding unnecessary expenses, the organization can achieve sustainable growth. We will explore the principles of effective budgeting and resource allocation and the strategies for managing cash flow and controlling costs.

Furthermore, financial acumen extends to investment and risk management. The architect of abundance adopts a diversified investment portfolio, balancing risk and return to ensure long-term financial stability. By making informed investment decisions and proactively managing risks, the organization can achieve sustainable growth and resilience. This chapter delves into the principles of investment and risk management and the importance of seeking expert advice when necessary.

15

Chapter 15: Visionary Thinking: Anticipating the Future

Visionary thinking is a key quality of the architect of abundance. The ability to anticipate future trends and opportunities is what sets successful leaders apart. This chapter explores the principles of visionary thinking and the steps necessary to build a forward-looking and innovative organization.

Visionary thinking begins with a commitment to continuous learning and curiosity. The architect of abundance stays informed about emerging trends and developments, seeking out new ideas and perspectives. By fostering a culture of curiosity and encouraging team members to explore new possibilities, the organization can remain agile and responsive to change. In this chapter, we delve into the strategies for cultivating visionary thinking within an organization and the importance of staying informed and adaptable.

Moreover, visionary thinking involves strategic foresight and planning. The architect of abundance adopts a long-term perspective, setting goals and strategies that anticipate future opportunities and challenges. By regularly reviewing and adjusting their plans, the organization can stay ahead of the curve and capitalize on emerging trends. We will explore the principles of strategic foresight and the strategies for effective long-term planning and goal-setting.

Furthermore, visionary thinking extends to innovation and creativity. The architect of abundance encourages a culture of innovation, where team members feel empowered to experiment, take risks, and explore new ideas. By fostering an environment that celebrates creativity and values diverse perspectives, the organization can drive innovation and stay ahead of the competition. This chapter delves into the principles of innovation and creativity and the strategies for fostering a culture of visionary thinking.

16

Chapter 16: Cultural Influence: Shaping the Zeitgeist

Cultural influence is a powerful tool for building an enduring empire. The architect of abundance understands the importance of shaping the cultural zeitgeist and creating a positive impact on society. This chapter explores the principles of cultural influence and the steps necessary to build a brand that resonates with people and shapes the cultural landscape.

Cultural influence begins with a commitment to authenticity and purpose. The architect of abundance prioritizes creating a brand that reflects their vision and values, resonating with people on a deeper level. By telling a compelling brand story and staying true to their principles, the organization can build a loyal following and create a lasting impact. In this chapter, we delve into the strategies for building a culturally influential brand and the importance of authenticity and purpose.

Moreover, cultural influence involves leveraging media and communication channels to amplify the organization's message. The architect of abundance adopts a strategic approach to media and communication, ensuring that their message reaches the right audience and creates a positive impact. By leveraging social media, traditional media, and other communication channels, the organization can shape public perception and drive cultural change. We will explore the principles of effective communication and the strategies for leveraging media to build cultural influence.

Furthermore, cultural influence extends to thought leadership and advocacy. The architect of abundance positions themselves as a thought leader and advocate for positive change, using their platform to inspire and influence others. By contributing to important conversations and championing social and environmental causes, the organization can create a positive impact and shape the cultural zeitgeist. This chapter delves into the principles of thought leadership and advocacy and the strategies for leveraging cultural influence to drive positive change.

17

Chapter 17: Conclusion: The Eternal Blueprint

The journey of building an enduring empire is one of vision, dedication, and unwavering commitment to creating value for future generations. The architect of abundance understands that true wealth lies not in the accumulation of riches, but in the lasting impact they create on the world. This chapter reflects on the principles and practices explored throughout the book and emphasizes the importance of building a legacy that outlasts generations.

The conclusion reiterates the key themes of the book, highlighting the importance of vision, innovation, ethical leadership, and community engagement in building a sustainable and prosperous empire. The architect of abundance recognizes that the journey is ongoing, and the blueprint for success is ever-evolving. By staying true to their vision and values, embracing change, and continuously striving for excellence, they can build an empire that endures through the ages.

The architect of abundance leaves behind a legacy of abundance, not just in material wealth, but in the values, principles, and positive impact they have created. As future generations carry forward the vision and build upon the foundation laid by the architect, the empire continues to thrive and evolve, creating a lasting legacy that transcends time.

The Architect of Abundance: Building Empires That Outlast Generations

In a world where success is often measured by fleeting accomplishments, there are those who dream of creating a legacy that stands the test of time. "The Architect of Abundance" is a transformative guide for visionary leaders who aspire to build empires that outlast generations. This book delves into the principles and practices that form the blueprint for enduring success, drawing insights from history, modern-day success stories, and timeless wisdom.

From laying the first bricks of wealth to embracing innovation, strategic growth, and ethical leadership, each chapter offers a deep dive into the essential elements of building a prosperous and sustainable empire. Learn how to cultivate a cohesive team, implement sustainable practices, and leverage technological advancements to stay ahead of the curve. Discover the importance of nurturing relationships, engaging with the community, and preparing the next generation to carry forward the legacy.

With a focus on resilience, visionary thinking, and cultural influence, "The Architect of Abundance" provides a comprehensive roadmap for leaders who seek to create a positive and lasting impact on the world. Whether you're an entrepreneur, business leader, or aspiring changemaker, this book will inspire you to think beyond immediate gains and build a legacy that endures through the ages.

www.ingramcontent.com/pod-product-compliance
Lightning Source LLC
LaVergne TN
LVHW020458080526
838202LV00057B/6025